I Just Came for the Candy

Candy

by Anita Hulshof

DEDICATION

Dedicated to the adults who made a positive impact
in Adam's life... you know who you are.

And to those who didn't... you know who you are,
too.

Introduction

When confronted with the realization that your child has a disability, you experience a jumble of emotions, from denial to acceptance as you grieve the life you imagined for your child to accepting the reality of what it will be. The feeling that stays with me forever is hope. I take you on this journey of my often frustrating, sometimes delightful and always wondrous life with my only son, Adam, in aspiring to keep that hope alive for us, and others who are traveling the difficult road of autism with us. This isn't meant to be a guide of how to navigate the world of autism, but merely a story of one family's struggles and joys of living with it. I hope to educate family and friends of some of the myths of autism, as well as showing other autism families that they are not alone. The message in church today was about seeing the light in the darkness. I hope Adam's story brings light. Although I've been writing this book "in my head" for quite some time, I have recently decided to make a serious effort to finish it. I am very open about my experiences in social media, and was informed a few days ago that Adam's progress has been encouraging to others.

Autism is not a behavior problem, although autistic kids can certainly have behavior problems. I think my dear friend, April Fox, who has been on this same journey longer than I have, said it best with the cards she made bearing this quote. "My son has autism. He is not stupid or undisciplined. Life for him can be overwhelming and scary. Imagine a hundred strangers talking to

you at once in a room with bright flashing lights.
That's how he feels in public a lot of the time.
You probably couldn't handle living in his world.
Please be understanding as he attempts to navigate
yours."

Sometimes you have the advantage of knowing in
advance that your child will have some type of
disability, and can counteract it to some extent,
or plan accordingly. Autism isn't one of those.
You find out as you are watching your child grow
and develop normally, and then stop, only to
regress, in many cases deep into their own world.
Experts say that early intervention is the key to
helping these special children, but it's not
always that easy to find those resources, and they
are not always available to parents. 1 in 59
children is now diagnosed with autism, and that
number is growing. There is no known cause or
cure, although there are theories that suggest
vaccinations play a part as well as genetic
factors. A good source of information is
https://nationalautismassociation.org/resources/au
tism-fact-sheet/. Another one is
https://www.tndisability.org/support-training-
exceptional-parents-inc They have a very good
handbook containing all kinds of resources. It is
good to have this book handy when attending IEP
meetings. I suggest doing your own research as
well.

Autism is described on a spectrum, from very high
functioning to severe. Some children are non-
verbal, but otherwise very intelligent. I feel
fortunate that Adam's type of autism, Pervasive
Developmental Disorder—Not Otherwise Specified
(PDD-NOS) isn't typically as severe as what is
defined as classic autism, although for some kids,
there can be debilitating symptoms. He is a very
bright and funny sixteen year old high school
junior, who sees the world through a different
lens than most of us. I have collected many of his
thoughts he shares with me when we are driving

somewhere, eating supper, or just hanging out.
Many of my friends refer to these as "Adamisms". I
will be sharing these here, as well.

The title of this book *I Just Came For The Candy*
came from Adam's dislike of parades. I encouraged
him to attend the local Christmas parade with me
one year. He wanted to leave immediately, so I
asked him why he bothered to come. He simply said,
"I just came for the candy."

CHAPTER 1

My late husband, Bobby, the father of my children, was a very sick man. Exactly how sick we wouldn't know until much later than his original diagnosis. He was diagnosed with Multiple Sclerosis, and was becoming more and more disabled each day. Because our lives weren't chaotic enough with medical appointments, running a household and raising our then ten-year-old daughter, Ainsley, it was during this time that we decided to have another baby. After suffering a miscarriage, I later gave birth to Adam on a balmy Flag Day, the day that Ainsley was to return home from summer camp. Many would question the sanity of adding to our family at that time, but for us, it was the right thing to do. With Bobby's health deteriorating, I was concerned that if anything happened to me, Ainsley would be left to shoulder the burden of taking care of her dad alone. Our hope was that a sibling would help share that burden. Little did we know then what his purpose would come to be.

There were no red flags in Adam's earliest months to indicate that there was anything to be concerned about. He reached all milestones on time. It wasn't until a well baby checkup somewhere between eighteen and twenty-four months that things started changing. When asked the usual questions about speech and behavior, I realized that perhaps there were some delays, but nothing that I felt was significant. Just after Adam's first birthday, Bobby suffered a stroke, and my time and attention had been on helping him through his recovery, and I might not have been as alert to things as I would have otherwise. Mommy guilt is a powerful thing, even when you know you are not at fault… at the same time, it pushes you to find the answers.

We later learned that Bobby's health problems were related to his heart and circulatory system. It was during his recovery process that I began to understand Adam's purpose for being here. He was sent for healing… for Bobby, as well as the many patients Adam visited every day when we went to see Bobby while he was in the nursing home. Unlike many toddlers, Adam wasn't afraid of strangers, and welcomed a hug or a pat on the head as he made his way down the hall until he reached his father's room.

I didn't think too much about Adam's habit, as a toddler, of lining up his toy cars and lying on the floor looking at the wheels. I just thought of it as a "boy thing" since I had only raised a girl to about twelve or thirteen years at that point. It was only later that I learned that it was a typical trait of autism. He knew more about cars as a two year old as anyone I'd ever seen, and knew what type of vehicle everyone he was familiar with drove, after seeing it only one time. Obsessions are often found in people with autism, although they can exchange one obsession for another after a period of time. He traded his car obsession with the popular Transformer toys and later on went on to video games. Having autism might also explain his custom as a young child of sleeping with a blanket over his head to block out distracting sights and sounds. One friend, who came to babysit, became concerned enough of him suffocating himself that she removed the blanket. He simply covered himself up again and went back to sleep.

At the encouragement of the pediatrician, Adam was evaluated by therapists at the Child Development

Center, a facility in our town that provides early intervention for young children with developmental delays or disabilities. It was determined there that he did have some delays in speech, and his fine motor skills, which also can be an indicator of autism. He attended twice a week for several months for therapy, as well as developing socialization skills, which are often lacking in autistic children, although at the time, we still didn't have a formal diagnosis of autism.

Adam continued to be a bright, playful, stubborn, happy, perfectly normal little boy, as he left toddlerhood and entered preschool age. We learned about Head Start, a preschool program for low income and special needs children, and I decided to apply for it to allow for more socialization with his peers. He did very well at first, and then became bored and disruptive. He refused to lie down at naptime and often was running around the classroom while his classmates were lost in blissful slumber. Others still were more concerned about his deficits than I was. It didn't seem important whether he used utensils or not, as long as he was able to feed himself. His speech as a three-year-old was more endearing than concerning and we still refer to Kid Cuisines, a frozen dinner marketed for children, as "Quigglezines".

CHAPTER 2

As Adam finished his term at Head Start, we began looking forward to kindergarten. He passed the readiness assessment, with acknowledgement of some seemingly minor deficits, that we hoped would be corrected as he learned and matured. Only a few weeks into the semester, however, there were problems. He was disruptive in class, refused to participate, and was a general nuisance. I was called to the school over and over again. I didn't understand why they couldn't work with him, as I had very little trouble with him at home. This, of course, was before his diagnosis and my understanding that these were all signs of autism. And then he was moved to another school into a behavior modification program for the remainder of kindergarten and well into first grade.

I had begun to accept that there was something wrong, but I had no clue as to what it was. At home, we were just like any other family, but when it was time to get out the door to go to school, it became a nightmare. He would pull off his shoes and socks, screaming that he could feel crumbs. I searched and paid way too much for seamless socks. That only worked temporarily because they didn't make them in larger sizes. As much as some people hate Crocs, they were a godsend for shoes, since he would at least have something on his feet. He became known as the boy who wore Crocs with his shorts or sweatpants. I gave up on trying to get him into jeans or other pants. If he was uncomfortable, he was not going to cooperate. I learned to pick my battles.

We continued to look for ways to get him diagnosed. We didn't have insurance, and child therapy is not cheap. Finally, one of his teachers gave me a pamphlet for a research study at Vanderbilt University on autism. So not only was he going to get a diagnosis, and we didn't have to pay, they would be paying us! The study required the entire family to participate, first with hours of questionairres, followed by observation of Adam by the researcher, then the four of us had blood drawn, pictures taken, as well as measurements of our hands and feet. This study was looking for a genetic link in autism families.

I had mixed emotions about the diagnosis. First, there was relief that we knew the reason for all of the behaviors, but sadness that things most people find easy would always be challenging to him. I also felt like the diagnosis would get him services for the help he needed to succeed in school. That's how it's supposed to work, anyway. He was moved once again to a different school, where he would receive different therapies (behavioral, occupational) as well as an assistant in the classroom. It was always my goal to have Adam attend regular mainstream classes as much as possible, as outlined by special education laws. Unfortunately, it didn't work that way, as I learned that there is a lack of autism education in our local school district, and Adam continued to be treated as a behavior problem.

In kindergarten he was confined to the bathroom with the behavior teacher sitting at the open door to keep him from running all around the room. I was uneasy about this arrangement, but I didn't

know of any alternatives, so I let it go. But then
one day when I went to pick him up, I was told
that he deliberately broke the toilet. He
repeatedly banged the seat down and he told his
teacher he wanted to break it and she basically
told him to do it, so he did. Bobby offered to pay
for the damage, but I only agreed to pay for half.
I believe in taking responsibility for my
children's actions, but I didn't think we should
be totally liable for something that happened
while he was under direct supervision of another
adult. The school superintendent said they would
send us a bill, but they never did. I believed it
was because they realized we could have actually
sued them if he had been injured as a result.

My days consisted of phone calls from the school,
followed by IEP (Individualized Education Program)
meetings. Once a child is identified with a
disability, they may have an IEP, and it MUST be
followed, as it is a legal document. This is where
you hear the words "least restrictive
environment", which is what is supposed to be
provided. To me, it meant that he would be allowed
to attend regular classes with regular kids, but
it was a long time before that would happen. I
hated those meetings, I always felt intimidated,
with all the "experts" on one side of the table,
and I was all alone. They always say you are part
of "the team", but in reality, they already know
what they want to do, and in many cases, pressure
you to agree.

Once we had a plan, he was placed in another
behavior program, where he was bullied by other
kids, as well as adults. On a field trip to the
zoo, he had a meltdown, and rather than have
adults to calm and comfort him, he was ridiculed
and told to "stop acting like a baby". He was
often excluded and missed many holiday parties at
school. He was even left out of Special Olympics!
On one occasion, he was excluded from a short
field trip in town, when all of the students were

taken to visit the school they would be attending
the following year as they were promoted. I worked
as an assistant at his school that year, and was
to escort him on this trip, but at the last
minute, I was told he would not be going, and was
not joining his class at the new school. I
insisted that he was going if I had to put him in
my car and drive him myself, but I grabbed his
hand and we ran down the hall and made it on the
bus just before it drove off. I was furious and
probably could have lost my job as a result, but I
had to stand up for my child. He moved on with his
class the next year at my insistence, but our
fight wasn't over. I thought my working at his
school would be good for him, but it actually
worked against him, so when I wasn't rehired for
the next year, I moved on to other things. I had
considered home schooling, but I always felt that
socialization, which I could not provide for him
at home, is as important as academics.

After many many suspensions, both in and out of
school, the situation was not improving. I
wholeheartedly believe that there is a lack of
autism training in our school district, especially
at the elementary level, and with so many new
diagnoses, it is imperative that they get on
board. I was becoming more and more frustrated and
angry at the school system for not understanding
his triggers. One day, while I was working after I
left my job with the school district, my mom
called to tell me the principal called her. My
parents were my much needed backup people for
times I wasn't available. She said she was told
that his nose was bleeding and he would have to go
home unless he had a clean shirt. My mom was
perplexed, but she drove up to the school with 3
clean t-shirts for him to choose from. When she
walked down the hall to his classroom, he was
lying on the floor screaming and moaning, with 3
adults hovering over him. She couldn't understand
why they didn't just back off and give him some
space to calm himself down. She said she would be

in the office with the shirts when he was ready.
After a few minutes, he came in, picked a shirt,
changed and returned to class. That, my friends,
is autism training. One teacher called him out in
class for not paying attention, which almost
always triggered a meltdown. She didn't understand
that eye contact is very difficult for autistic
people, and just because he wasn't looking at her
didn't mean he wasn't paying attention. He learned
by listening and could excel on any test after
hearing the material one time. I was blamed for my
parenting and made to feel like his behavior was
my fault. Nevertheless, we moved forward.

CHAPTER 3

The year Adam turned eight, Bobby's health took a turn for the worse, and he passed away. I was truly now on my own in advocating for my child, although Bobby never really gave a lot of input, he was still always in agreement with me in fighting for our son. Although my family openly discussed our loss, it was three years before most of the teachers and other adults who dealt with Adam on a regular basis were aware of it. I brought it up at an IEP meeting to have his name removed from his paperwork. The gasps around the table were audible, as I was shocked that no one ever bothered to talk to this child to understand what was going on in his mind. This meeting was also when the principal and counselor broke into giggling fits when I told them about Adam's gastrointestinal issues, which is common in autistic kids, thought to be a consequence of food aversions, due to texture and other reasons. It often resulted in him soiling his pants and I wanted the team to be aware that it could be a problem. One assistant at the elementary school actually accused him of doing it deliberately, so he started trying to hold it in, so she wouldn't yell at him for asking to go to the bathroom. That only led to more accidents. I realized later that I should have spoken up at the meeting, because I filed a complaint with the school board, and was told that since the special education director didn't see it, it didn't happen. I was simply too upset to speak at the time.

It was during this time period when I learned I would have to be my own advocate. At each IEP meeting, you are given a booklet of your child's "rights" as a special needs student. Included are

resources for attorneys and advocacy groups in the
event that you are facing issues that you cannot
resolve on your own. When it was suggested that
Adam be moved to the middle school (6th and 7th
grade in our school district), as a fifth grader,
I resisted. I didn't feel that Adam was mature
enough to handle being with much older kids. I
spoke with several advocates about how to handle
it, and although I was given some good advice, I
was still on my own when it came to speaking out
at the meetings. I filed for due process, which
means you meet with all parties involved, with or
without attorneys to work things out. The school
board was able to outlawyer me, and I eventually
gave in. I believed he wasn't receiving any
education where he was, so it couldn't be any
worse. Except it was.

Any time there is a change in "services", it has
to be reflected in the IEP, and there is a
meeting. Once I accepted the fact that Adam was
going to be moved to the middle school, we had
that meeting. I always want them to know about his
triggers, so the possibility of a meltdown is
lessened. I told them of a particular child who
pushes his buttons, so they could limit contact
between the two of them. I was assured they would
do all they could to keep things running as
smoothly as possible. Except they didn't. I left
that meeting with tears in my eyes, after
listening to adults giggling like little girls,
and offering me no hope. When the principal asked
me if I was ok, I just nodded, when I should have
said "no, I'm not ok, I just sold my son out". But
they gave me no choice.

CHAPTER 4

A few weeks after the transition, I was called for
an emergency meeting. He apparently pushed a table
and it struck his teacher, leaving a large bruise
on her side. I asked what triggered this event,
and was told that the child he has problems with
was sitting near him and he exploded, and was
taken to another room, where, once again, adults
were hovering over him, escalating the situation.
I reminded the teacher and special education
director that I had warned them that the other
child was a trigger for him, and I was told that I
couldn't dictate where another child sat. I wasn't
asking for that, I just wanted him to have the
abilty to leave the situation before it got out of
control, and he was denied that option. I do have
to say that the other child was doing nothing
wrong, but just being near him is like nails on a
chalkboard to Adam.

I was called to meet with the team the next day
for a manifestation determination. Manifestation
determination is a test employed when a student
who receives special education services is
considered for suspension, expulsion or any

alternative placement due to some behavioral
concern. ... (II) if the conduct in question was
the direct result of the local educational
agency's failure to implement the IEP. In other
words, they decide if the action was a result of
the disabilty. I believed it was, but they
disagreed and deemed him a violent thug. The
teacher mentioned counseling, but I didn't think
it was appropriate for him, he didn't need to be
counseled for the school's inability to teach
autistic kids.

A few days later, I answered the door to a
sheriff's deputy, serving me with a summons to
appear in court. Adam was being charged with
assault. Needless to say, I was very upset. I
called one of the advocates I spoke with
previously when they were forcing him to change
schools. She agreed with me that they were wrong,
but really, there was nothing I could do until the
court date, and speak for Adam.

Within a couple of weeks, I was doing some work at
home when the phone rang. It was Adam's teacher
telling me that she was having problems with him
and she didn't know what to do. I told her I would
come to the school, so I put away the things I was
working on, and headed to town. I was so angry
that they insisted on putting him in this
situation, but had no idea how to handle him.
Stress tends to bring out the worst in people, and
all of this was incredibly stressful to me, so
didn't have the best reaction. I went into his
classroom and told the teacher to prepare his work
through the end of the year, I would take him home
and teach him. Then I went home and had my own
meltdown.

I knew he had to go to school, I had the court
date coming up and I just made things worse. I
called my advocate and told her what happened, and
although she sympathized with me, she agreed that

he needed to get back in school. I returned him
the next week with the completed work.

I found a wonderful counselor who works with
children on the autism spectrum and made an
appointment before the court date. She couldn't
understand why he was there, she didn't see any
issues with him, but we did what we had to do. I
wasn't happy with the court proceeding. The judge
was not sympathetic to Adam's disability, and said
he has to learn to deal with others. I argued that
was why he was in a behavior program, so he could
be taught that. Ultimately, her decision was to
send him to counseling for a year, with regular
reports to the court, and if there were no more
incidents, the assault would be removed from his
record. There weren't, so we moved forward.

At the end of the school year, parents were
instructed to pick up their child's report card at
the appropriate school. Adam's grades were good,
but what caught my attention was the certificate
of achievement included. I don't remember what it
was for, but I know I cried.

CHAPTER 5

The next hurdle would be finding an acceptable placement for eighth grade. I was not about to send him back to the middle school where he had such a horrible experience. I began looking into homeschooling, but kept running into dead ends in transferring his records, and my heart wasn't really in it anyway. I still wanted him to be with other kids. I also want the doubters to see him walk across that stage to accept his dipoloma. It was during this period that I learned that there was a new special education director for the district. I didn't know whether to be happy or worried, but they couldn't be any worse than the last one.

It turned out she was a godsend. I told her all of my concerns and all of the things Adam had been through, as much as I could without sobbing. She understood. She actually understood! And she promised it would get better. So a meeting was scheduled with the team to decide what the next step would be. I still was apprehensive of her suggestion of moving Adam to the high school in eighth grade, but she assured me it would work out. The principal, counselors and other members of the team were kind and reassuring. For the first time in his life, I felt positive about Adam's education.

The principal, counselors, and the special education director for the high school were wonderful. I was especially pleased that the principal told me that he has a family member on the spectrum, so he understands.

There were still problems, issues, and phone calls. I started calling the director every time a teacher called me, and she handled it immediately. The calls became fewer and farther between. One incident that stands out with a particular teacher was when Adam was having a meltdown for some reason. Kids were allowed to bring their hand held games or phones and play with them on break times. He was upset and threw his game, and the teacher, rather than diffusing the situation, told Adam to go ahead and keep throwing it, his mom would buy him another one. I was, once again livid that this wasn't handled appropriately, showing once again, the lack of training for autistic kids. Another time, an assistant told Adam that he had been kidnapped because I picked him up early for a dentist appointment, rather than his usual routine of riding the bus, and she didn't recognize my handwriting on the sign out sheet.

Still, it continued to get better. Adam was finally coming out of his shell, and made friends. He warmed up to the new special education teacher and did most of his work without any problems.

CHAPTER 6

Freshman year seemed to be pivotal for Adam. He made a lot of progress in academics, as well as behavior, although I had my doubts at the beginning. I attended back to school night with Adam. We listened to the "welcome back" speeches, and then were instructed to find their classrooms and meet the teachers. As we navigated the crowded hallways, I could only think how was he going to do this every day? I held it together until we met the wonderful art teacher he later formed a bond with. She assured me everything would be ok, and for the most part, it was. She became the go-to person when no one else could calm him down, and although she later resigned her position, we still keep in contact with her.

I was still emotional when we met his homeroom teacher. She was also reassuring and kind, and when he later was in her criminal justice classes, had nothing but praise for him.

I felt like we made it over the hurdle the first time Homecoming rolled around. Adam knows it's a trigger for him. All of the activity and commotion is unnerving to him, so he wanted to stay home. I told him if it was okay with the principal, I was fine with it. So he took it upon himself and asked, and was granted permission. After that, he continued to recognize his triggers and take charge. If he feels he is losing control, he goes to a designated room. I very rarely now get any phone calls from the school, and when I do, they tell me what happened and how it was handled.

Although I have written about many many incidents at school, that's not to say there haven't been some at home. There are broken doors and furniture in my house, and we have had a call to the sheriff's office, but these episodes are pretty rare and usually end pretty quickly.

At every IEP meeting, I am asked what my goals are for Adam, and it's always the same. I want him to graduate on time, with his class with a regular diploma. He is on track to do exactly that. In fact, there is a possiblity that he could graduate a semester early. As I finish these last pages, we are home on a stay home order due to the Covid - 19 outbreak, so it is subject to change.

I wrote this book, not to put Adam in the spotlight, because he will surely hate that, but to emphasize the need for autism training in public schools. I can't pretend to know what hte future holds for him, but I do know he will graduate. And I will cry. Whatever he decides to do, or if his limitations keep him from holding a job, I will always have his back. As difficult as it might be, I urge parents of these wonderful young people to fight, no matter how much resistance there is. You know what is best for your child!

Adamisms

Answers by Adam, age five and a half.

This is a cute idea. Copy this note, ask your child the questions and write them down exactly how they respond. Tag me back if you have done this, I'd love to hear the answers.

1. What is something mom always says to you? Clean up your room!

2. What makes mom happy? Cleaning up my room.

3. What makes mom sad? Not cleaning up my room.

4. How does your mom make you laugh? Putting 7 dishes on my head and balancing them on my head.

5. What was your mom like as a child? A little girl.

6. How old is your mom? Fifty-sixty-eight.

7. How tall is your mom? 12 inches.

8. What is her favorite thing to do? Work on the computer and print what she wants to print.

9. What does your mom do when you're not around? Work on her computer.

10. If your mom becomes famous, what will it be
for? Playing a guitar and disguising as a boy.

11. What is your mom really good at? Disguising as
a boy.

12. What is your mom not very good at? Disguising
as a girl. (because you're already a girl)

13. What does your mom do for her job? Get money.

14. What is your mom's favorite food? Hamburger
helper. Am I right on that one?

15. What makes you proud of your mom? Playing in
the living room without yelling.

16. If your mom were a cartoon character, who
would she be? One of the autobots.

17. What do you and your mom do together? Play
with toy cars.

18. How are you and your mom the same? Nuffin.

19. How are you and your mom different? Nuffin. Am
I correct on bofe of those?

20. How do you know your mom loves you? By playing
on the ceiling.

21. Where is your mom's favorite place to go? Let
me guess... Arby's. Is that correct?

Wednesday, March 18, 2009

Adam: Mom?

Me: What?

Adam: I think I'm pretty powerful.

Me: Ok.

trying to explain to Adam how to graciously accept
a gift at the school Christmas party tomorrow...
"No meltdowns, even if it's something you don't
like, or someone else gets something you think is
better". His reply... "What if it's made in
China?" 12/16/2009

Adam: Is a bunion an onion that grows on your
foot? 12/11/2009

Adam, while looking at new calendar... 16 months?!
Are they changing it? 12/18/2009

Deck the halls of owls of holly, fa la la la la la
la la la. 12/20/2009

Me: How much toilet paper did you use? Adam: Just
2 rolls. I'm gonna be busy for a while. 12/28/2009

Adam: Men are manly and do not want ponies.
1/2/2010

Adam: Am I cute even if I eat too much junk food?
1/8/2010

Adam: 3 + 3 = 6 licks. That seemed to motivate me.
1/13/2010

Adam: Can we watch Underdog tomorrow? Me: If you
clean up your toys, I might watch it with you.
Adam: I guess I have to watch it by myself.
1/31/10

Adam: "I will jump til my eyes fall out." 2/14/10

Adam: "I think I took a drink of funny sauce."
2/28/10

Adam: It would be really annoying if.... wait, I
AM really annoying! 3/19/10

Adam: You know what's weirder and grosser than Ainsley and me? Roasting pickles! 3/19/10

Adam: I'm full of surprises, ain't I? 3/25/10

Me: Adam, what's that all over the floor? Adam: I bet you're wondering, right? 3/31/10

Adam: My eyes almost throwed up when I looked at her (Ainsley). 4/7/10

Me: You have cooties and you stink. Adam: The stink part is correct. 5/3/10

Adam: Flowers are gonna be..... oh, wait, that's supposed to be a surprise. 5/7/10

Me: I'm so DONE with you! Adam: And the day has just started. 6/4/10

Adam: What's a bartender? Me: Someone who pours drinks. Adam: Can I have a drink? Am I a bartender? 6/17/10

Adam: "I might be a teenager by 2019. <blink, blink>" 6/24/10

Adam: When were computers invented? Me: I'm not sure, why? Adam: Whenever they did it, they did a pretty good job. 6/24/10

Me: Adam, are you being a pain? Adam: No, I'm being a veterinarian!.... Of course I'm being a pain! 6/24/10

Adam: When I'm 22, will I have to shop for you? I can buy you meat products. 6/27/10

Adam: I don't have dreams... I have nightmares. 7/6/10

Adam: It's a good thing my nose is stopped up. Me: Why? Adam: I farted. 7/7/10

Me: I know all about kids making up stuff. Adam:
Except for me, sometimes I tell the truth. 7/22/10

Adam: Is my plumber cracking? 7/27/10

Adam: If you're still alive when I'm 29, I'll come
visit you. 8/2/10

Me: I'm gonna sell you to the gypsies. Adam: I
need to bring my toys.... and diapers. Me:
Diapers?! Adam: Yeah, in case someone has a
baby... or do gypsies lay eggs? 8/16/10

"I pledge all agents, to the flag, of the United
States of America..." ~Adam 8/30/10

Adam (holding packet of taco seasoning mix) : "How
do you make tacos out of THIS? 9/9/10

Adam: I'm almost dressed, I just don't have any
pants on. 10/4/10

Adam: Can I buy a convertible when I get older?
Me: Yeah, will you let me drive it? Adam: Sure, if
you're not dead by then. 10/7/10

Adam: Why were those guys looking for chili in
that mine? 10/13/10

Adam, after waking up from a 2 hour nap : I was
NOT asleep! 10/14/10

Adam: What's for supper? Me: Lasagna. Adam: I hope
Garfield doesn't show up. 10/14/10

Adam: You're going to have to re-potty train me. I
stand up to pee. 10/20/10

Adam: What's that smell? Me: You. Adam: No, I mean
it smells good. 10/26/10

Adam: Sometimes I don't think Santa exists. Me: Why? Adam: Sometimes we get cheap stuff that only you would get. 11/1/10

Adam: I'll be glad when this election stuff is over, so we can stop worrying about who is going to steal all the money. 11/2/10

Me: See if you can keep your shirt clean until after you get your pict... what is that all over your shirt?! Adam: Boogers. 11/2/10

Adam: I have a good life. 11/4/10

Adam: why do I have to have such an obnoxious sister? 11/8/10

Adam: Have you ever heard of Thinkway Toys? Me: No. Adam: I haven't heard of it either. 11/9/10

Adam: When I grow up, I want to be a popsicle. Me: You want to be a popsicle?! Adam: What I meant to say was, I want to be a movie star. 11/11/10

Me: ARGH! You drive me nuts, boy, NUTS!! Adam: Bwahahahahaaa, say that again! Me: Why do you want me to yell at you? Adam: Cause it was funny this time. 11/11/10

Adam: What's wrong with that bus? There must be a scientific explanation! 11/11/10

Adam: when I am older, you know what I might start my day with? Me: What? Adam: A cup of coffee 11/16/10

Adam: when I get older, I will adopt some kids... or how else do you get some kids? oh, you can get married and get her to have some. 11/16/10

Adam: I was born in Stupidland! 11/17/10

Ainsley: Some of these players have butts. Adam:
They all have butts. 11/21/10

Adam: MAKE ME LUNCH! Me: It's not lunchtime yet.
Adam: Fine! I'll make my own in the oven. Me: Ok.
Adam: I don't know how to cook. 11/24/10

Adam: It didn't break, ok? Ok? Ok? Ok? 11/24/10

Adam: Do you still have the Santa cup? Me: What
Santa cup? Adam: The one with Santa on it.
11/24/10

Adam: Mistletoe? Is that what that is? Me: Yes, do
you know what that's for? Adam: Kissing.... but I
hope I don't end up with Mackenzie under there...
why do they call it mistle... that sounds like a
dangerous weapon... I guess it is. 11/24/10

Adam: What kind of crazy shows did they have back
then? 11/25/10

Me: It's almost time to go and you're not even
dressed. Adam: Is that a problem? 11/30/10

Adam: That cloud looks like an alligator fighting
an old man in the shower. 12/2/10

Adam: I'm just here for the candy. 12/4/10

Adam: Rodeo? That's a stupid name for a car.
12/4/10

Adam: I miss Ainsley. 12/8/10

Adam: I have a question. Me: I have an answer.
Adam: What? Me: No. 12/09/10

Adam: This firefighter has a buff chest. I think
girls might be attracted to him. 12/10/10

Adam: I hate you. Me: Good, that means I'm doing
my job. Adam: I love you. 12/13/10

Adam: My private spot hurts. Me: Why? Adam: I've been playing with it. 12/16/10

Me: WhatEVERRRRR! Adam: You sound just like Ainsley. 12/17/10

Adam: Daddy bought some gummies yesterday but he wouldn't let me have them yet. Me: That's between you and him. I'm not getting involved. Adam: Just get involved. 12/19/10

Bobby: Why do you like those Transformers so much? Adam: Autism. 12/21/10

Adam: Why don't cats like blanket? Well, they like them, they just don't like them on their heads. 12/22/10

Adam: Do you text? Me: Yes, I do. Adam: That's weird. 12/22/10

Adam: We're going to get up at 5am on Saturday, right? 12/23/10

Adam: I'm going to move away, far away from Ainsley 12/20/10

Adam: Should we turn off the fireplace tonight? Me: Uh, why? Adam: Fat man? Sneaking in to give us presents? Sheesh! 12/24/10

Adam: "I don't know and I don't care is your catch phrase?" 12/27/10

Adam: This is the time I wish I had a brother, cause Teddy won't play with me cause he's a cat. 12/27/2010

Adam: Teddy is kneading on my private spot. It feeeels gooooood. <giggle> 12/28/10

Adam: Sometimes I think I'm speaking a language I don't know. 12/29/10

Adam: Are you tired? Me: Yes. Adam: Of what, me? 12/29/10

Adam: When are you going to feed Dodger? Me: Soon. Adam: He's starving! In dog years, it's been 5 hours!   12/30/10

Adam: Mom, you're embarrassing me. 12/30/10

Adam: Remember when we stayed up til midnight and cheered for the new year? Me: Yes, I remember, it was only a few hours ago. Adam: Well, it was yesterday. No, technically it was today, the very first thing. 1/1/11

Adam: This is the best year ever! Even though it's just started, it's still the best year! 1/1/11

Adam: I feel so powered up that I can stay up all night. 1/2/11

Adam: Whatever you tell me to do, I do the opposite. 1/2/11

Adam: Dad's gone. Me: Then close the front door. Adam: Why, so he can't get back in? 1/3/11

Adam: Are you happy? Me: I'm deliriously happy. Adam: Why, 'cause Dad's gone? 1/3/11

Adam: It was Ainsley's idea to get him (Dodger), so we should ban her from the family. But not Dodger. 1/4/11

Adam: Ainsley, does this guy look cool? Does he look cool? Hey, is this Transformer cool? Hey! Hey! I'm TALKING to you!!! Ainsley: What?! Adam: Does this guy look cool? 1/7/11

Adam: Let me check if my pants are done leaking.
1/10/11

Adam: I'm not a brat, I have autism. Me: You are a
brat AND you have autism. 1/12/11

Me: That's what happens when you act stupid. Adam:
I'm not acting. 1/20/11

Adam: I accidentally threw your phone in the
garbage... you might want to clean it off. 1/20/11

Adam: I got through with the spoons, so I threw
them away. Grandma: You threw them away? Adam: No,
I put them in the sink, I get confused. Grandma:
We usually just wash them. 1/21/11

Adam: Don't worry, Goldie cleaned it up. 1/26/11

Adam: why would you want a mobile home if it
doesnt have a steering wheel? 1/31/11

Adam: I can turn any conversation into a different
one. 2/12/11

Adam: I sound like a monkey. Me: You smell like
one, too. Adam: That's my feet. 2/22/11

Me: I'm just getting here. Adam: What are you, a
turtle? 4/24/11

Adam: Look at that dog! Look at that dog! Look at
that dog! Look at that dog! You shoulda seen that
dog. 3/27/11

Adam: It must be hard being a mime. 3/28/11

Me: You're a bunch of pigs. Adam: No, I'm only one
pig. 3/28/11

Adam: That's the longest one I ever pooped out.
3/31/11

Adam: If we live on an old country road, why don't we talk like old country people? 4/2/11

Adam: Do they have cameras all over the place, even on the interstates? Me: Yup. Adam: I think we're being watched. 4/4/11

Adam: I think I finally reached puberty. 4/11/11

Adam: I'm weird, ain't I? 4/11/11

Adam: I'm secretly saying 'ow'. I guess it's not a secret anymore. 4/13/11

Adam: What's Dodger's whole name? Me: I don't know, the Artful Dodger? Adam: He doesn't paint! 4/13/11

Adam: Do you know how to tell a boy horse from a girl horse? The boy horse has shorter hair. 4/16/11

Me: Stop doing that. It makes me want to strangle you. Adam: Enough with the trash talk already. 4/27/11

Me: Turn off the tv and go to bed. Adam: Can't you say something nicer? 5/16/11

Me: Stop squeaking. Adam: It's not squeaking, it's a farting sound. 5/18/11

Adam: what is this, hippie music? 5/18/11

Adam: If Grandma's home today, we could ask her to give us some lunch. 5/30/11

Adam: Do you know what I'm famous for? Me: Being a pain in the butt. Adam: I'm the best pain in the butt there is! 5/4/11
Adam: Can we have McDonald's for supper? Me: Quit asking me that. Adam: Well, will you answer with a "yes"? 6/1/11

Adam: What's for supper? Me: Cicada stew. Adam: I think I'll have McDonald's. 6/1/11

Adam: Are we...? Me: Don't ask me again. Adam: Can we still go to McDonald's? 6/1/11

Ainsley: The wasp isn't going to get you and if it did, you're not going to die. Adam: Yeah, but I'd cry uncontrollably. 6/3/11

Adam: I got monkey fever! 6/6/11

Adam: Maybe on Saturday I'll leave you alone the rest of the day... maybe.... not sure... 6/6/11

Adam: I like disturbing you! 6/10/11

Adam: Your privacy is not my privacy. Me: Really? Adam: Yeah. Me: What does that even mean? Adam: I don't know, you'll know in a few minutes. 6/22/11

Adam: Whatever you do, take me where you go, unless I can't go with you. 6/24/11

Adam: I definitely know you do not like Transformers. 6/25/11

Adam: It's never too late for grape juice! 6/30/11

I told Adam to tell you thanks for dinner and he asked if you paid and I said yes, I have the card and he said "smart plan, twisted, but smart" (Ainsley) 7/10/11

Me: I want you to clean up your room, please. Adam: What's in it for me? 7/12/11

Adam: I don't know why I cried. It was like I was in a movie for a few minutes. 7/12/11

Adam: Did you eat that cookie? Me: No. Adam:
That's what happens in court. Suspects always say
no. 8/5/11

Adam: Are you going grocery shopping today? Me: I
don't know. Adam: I can help you with that
decision. 8/11/11

Adam: I'm not civilized. 8/12/11

Adam, to teacher at funeral home: Well, this is
awkward. 8/15/11

Me: I was so proud of you today. You did a great
job! Adam: I don't think you should be all that
proud. 8/16/11

Adam: I wish this was all a dream. You could call
it a nightmare. 8/16/11

Adam: I can't help but notice that Aunt Ruby found
her false teeth. 8/17/11

Adam: Why are you out here? Me: To enjoy the
quiet. Adam: You've come to the wrong place.
8/17/11

Adam: I don't have the diarrhea anymore, I just
have the pee-arrhea. 8/18/11

Adam: What if we had a voodoo doll of Mom? Imagine
what we could do then! Me: How do you know about
voodoo dolls? Adam: Well, I do watch a lot of
TV... 8/18/11

Adam: Once I invent a time machine, I'll show ya!
8/23/11

Adam: Rosie isn't skunky stinky now, she's just
regular stinky, can she come in? 8/8/11

Adam: Wow, this is award-winning fog! 8/22/11

Me: You're the biggest pain in the butt there is!
Adam: Well.... in the United States... 8/23/11

Adam: Footloose? It sounds like their shoes are
untied. 9/16/11

Adam: I'm gonna throw the wii in the garbage...
No, wait, that would be stupid. 12/14/2011

Adam: Interesting fact... Did you know that before
it was a bad word, it used to be called a donkey?
12/14/2011

Me: All I owe you is a roof over your head, food
to eat and clothes to wear. Adam: And
Transformers! 12/14/2011

Adam: I don't understand how a really big guy
could be coming down the chimney. 12/22/2011

Adam (setting out cookies for Santa) How many? Me:
2. Adam: He'll like 4. 12/24/2011

Adam: Hey, Mom? Me: What? Adam: I'm happy."
6/27/12

Adam: I don't like what you're making for supper.
I'm making something else. Me: This isn't a
restaurant. Adam: Duh, you don't make your own
food in a restaurant." 7/18/12

Adam: You turn blue, then you die. 8/6/12

Me: We're not pigs, it's about time we started
living like we're not. Adam: We all have our own
personalities. 8/8/12

Adam: Sometimes it's good when water comes out of
your nose.... you're gonna put this on that book
thing, aren't you? 8/8/12

Adam: YOU ALMOST SET THE HOUSE ON FIRE! Me: No, I
didn't, it just boiled over a little. Adam: Well,
you almost boiled the house to death." 8/8/12

Ainsley: There's an ambulance at McDonald's. Adam:
It's either a health attack, or someone is
pregnant, or someone is internally bleeding.
8/10/12

Adam: If you ever die, and you can't remember how
you died, ask me and I'll tell you. 8/10/12

Adam: I'm going to run into a lemon tree. Ainsley:
Why? Adam: If life gives you lemons, make
lemonade! 8/10/12

Ainsley: When you graduate, you get to live in the
real world. Adam: What? I live in the real world
now. 8/10/12

Me: You should ask Mackenzie to go with you to the
dj party at the end of the month. Adam: Will you
buy me a little tuxedo? 8/14/12

Adam: That's an unfortunate name for a valley...
Death Valley? I thought valleys were supposed to
be peaceful. 8/16/12

Adam: What I mean by "a lot" is "A LOT! 8/16/12

Adam: Mom, could you be a little less noisy about
it? I think the whole neighborhood can hear you.
8/25/12

Adam: I think people who are autistic like me
don't have normal heads. 9/5/12

Adam: Wouldn't it be nice if headlights lasted
forever? Me: It would be nice if lots of things
lasted forever. Adam: Like life? .... if it
weren't for Adam and Eve... not this Adam, the
other Adam, the first one. 9/7/12

Power went out briefly. Adam: MOM!!!... oh I just went blind for 5 seconds. 9/12/12

Adam: I don't really like vegetables, but I like broccoli, carrots and tomatoes 9/14/12

Adam: They don't need all those lights. They have headlights, unless they are going by horse and wagon. 9/15/12

Adam: You know those sweet potato fries? Me: Do they have them at school? Adam: Yeah, they're kinda gross, they might be better with marshmallows. 9/18/12

Adam: When Grandma's trees start hatching pears, can we have some? 9/21/12

Adam: Please don't hurt me, I'm too scared. 10/13/12

Adam: Mom? You used to look pretty good. 10/17/12

Adam: Well, dogs can't vote. 10/18/12

Adam: Does Canada have a language? Me: They speak English or French. Adam: And sometimes they say "eh". 10/18/12

Adam: This towel is kinda small, don't look, ok? 10/21/12

<phone rings> Ainsley: Let me talk to Adam. Adam: Whaaaaat? I don't want to talk to youuuuuu. 10/22/12

Me: I'm the bomb diggety. Adam: If you keep saying that, I am NOT going to high-five you. 10/23/12

Adam: Can you get me the new Skylanders game? How much money do you have? Try not to buy as much food. 10/27/12

Adam: If the tooth fairy doesn't come, can you just give me a dollar? Me: YES! 10/27/12

Adam: Rosie is having a seizure and bouncing like a gorilla. 10/29/12

Adam: Did you know that Santa, the tooth fairy, the sandman and the Easter bunny all know each other? 10/20/12

Adam: Mom, I don't want to talk about that anymore. 10/31/12

Adam: I want to get on your computer. Me: Ok, just be careful. Adam: HUH? What's going to happen? Me: I dunno, I'm delirious. 11/5/12

Me: ADAM! Adam: WHAT? Me: What are you doing? Adam: Picking my nose. 11/8/12

Me: Be quiet. Adam: I see you're extra mean today. 11/10/12

Adam: Mom? Me: What? Adam: Is that you? Me: No. Adam: Then why did you answer? 11/12/12

Me: Why would you you say something like that? Adam : Cause I'm just that crazy. 11/13/12

Me: Something stinks and it's you. Adam: Yup, it's me. 11/16/12

Me: God, something stinks! Adam: Don't talk about me. 11/16/12

Me: How did you get poop on the floor? Adam: Oh, I don't know. I really don't have an answer for that. 11/16/12

Adam: We finally get to meet a German! 11/22/12

Me: I've about had it with you and your big mouth.
Adam: My mouth is not big, it's normal-sized.
11/22/12

Adam: Rosie, just because you are deaf and blind
doesn't mean you have the right to lick my shorts.
11/24/12

Adam: This is the first time you made breakfast
casserole that it's actually good. Me: It's always
good. Adam: You made this before? Me: Yes. Adam:
Well, this is the first time you got it right.
11/24/12

Adam: I can't do everything at once. Me: Why not?
Adam: I'm not you. 11/24/12

Adam: Ewww, I licked his fur. Am I weird? I wanted
to see what Dizzy tastes when she massages Teddy.
11/25/12

Adam: You're watching church on tv? See, you don't
have to go to church to go to church. Me: Yeah,
but sometimes it's good to be with other people.
Adam: You are with other people. Teddy is
watching. 11/25/12

Me: I'm not going to Walmart. Adam: I KNOW! Black
Friday is still going on. 11/25/12

Adam: The Titans are done for. 11/25/12

Adam: If I'm imagining tiny kittens playing
football, it's just so cute. Imagine it. 11/25/12

Adam: Everything sounds funny in a language you
don't understand. 12/2/12

Adam: More people in Lewisburg don't believe in
Santa than do believe. I'm surprised he comes to
Lewisburg at all. I guess he just goes to the
houses that believe. 12/7/13

Adam: What happened to your voice? Me: Adam: No, it's not. Me: Adam: <giggle> 12/7/12

Adam: Well, it's time for spaghetti. 4:56 12/11/12

Adam downloaded the nice/naughty scanner on the kindle. It said "nice" for about 20 times that he tried it. The first time I did, it said "naughty" so he made me try it again, and then it said "nice". He said, "it had to check waaaaaaaaay back in your past. 12/24/12

Adam: Are you happy? Me: NO! Adam: Trick question, you're never happy. 12/24/12

Me: You've lived in this house as long as I have. Adam: No, I haven't. 12/30/12

Me: You need to take a bath tonight. Adam: WHY?? I took one a few days ago! 1/6/13

Me: An autistic girl is competing for Miss America. Do you know what that means? Autistic people can be anything they want to be. You, too, could be Miss America. Adam: That would be stupid. 1/12/13

Adam: Will you turn on the big light? Me: Why can't you? Adam: I can't reach it. Me: You just need to learn to me more... Adam: Tall? Me: Well, I was thinking... creative... innovative... resourceful... but yeah, that works. 1/15/13

Adam: I hate you. Me: Good. That means I'm doing my job. Adam: No, it means you're fired. Me: Does that mean you're moving out tonight? 1/16/13

Adam: 5 SECOND RULE! Ok, I know it's been updated to 3 seconds. It's a 2 second difference. 1/16/13

Me: What are you doing? Adam: Apparently, wasting time. 1/16/13

Me: You need to clean up after yourself. Adam:
I'll start when I'm 16. Me: If you don't start
now, you won't make it to 16. 1/31/13

Adam: You hate me. Me: Yes, I do. Adam: You don't
have to say it out loud. 2/1/13

Me, after realizing he never took his backpack out
of the van yesterday: I hope you didn't have any
homework. Adam: I don't know why you're still hung
up on that. 2/7/13

Me: Adam, STOP! Adam: Don't judge me. 2/16/13

Adam: You're obviously in a bad mood. Me: Yes, I
am. Adam: You don't have to state it, I already
know. 2/24/13

Adam: 4 weeks?! It didn't seem like 4 weeks, it
seemed like a month. 3/2/13

Adam: I can see the future. It's not a very good
future. I'll be a fat mechanic. 3/7/13

Adam: Caution, do not come in here! This is the
area where I've been farting. 3/20/13

Me: Did you take a shower? Adam: YES! Me: What did
you do with your dirty underwear? Adam: Oh... uh,
I didn't take a shower 3/21/13

Adam: I saw a ferry.... That's a ferry BOAT, not
the mythical creature... Just thought Mack should
know . 3/24/13

Adam: Mack is the one who makes them stink. I am
the one who makes them loud. 4/1/13

Mack: Eat right. Adam: My name's not Wright.
4/6/13

Adam: I'm happy today. 4/11/13

Adam: This tea was refreshing yesterday. Now it tastes like a hamburger. 4/18/13

Adam: Do I have to say final answer for you to write it down? 4/18/13

Adam: That sounds like a whale crossed with Scooby Doo. 4/19/13

Adam: Keith Urban does not sing to you! Me: Yes, he does. Adam: Prove it! Me: I don't have to prove it, I feel it in my heart. Adam: I know it in my head that he doesn't. 4/28/13

Adam: Are you crazy? Me: Just a little bit. Adam: No, you're a psychopath. 4/28/13

Adam: People are truly rich with tax. 5/3/13

Adam: I feel sorry for chickens... But they are delicious. 5/3/13

Ainsley: You are my minion. Adam: Can't you use a better word? 5/25/13

Me: I'm gonna take you and get your ears cleaned out. Adam: I don't need my eggs cleaned out. 5/25/13

Adam: I'm gonna come back and eat that in a minute. My stomach is kind of full, but not completely, I just need to wait for a burp. 5/29/13

Adam: I kinda like pork roast. I like anything that starts with pork or meat... pork ROAST, meat LOAF, Lasagne with MEAT and CHEESE. 5/30/13

Adam: Thank you. Me: You are not welcome at all.
Adam:HAHAHA, that's funny! That was a joke, wasn't
it? 6/2/13

Adam: Are you happy? Are you happy? Me: I won't be
happy until you be quiet. Adam: Then you'll never
be happy. 6/8/13

Adam: looks like I'm getting 2 cherries in one
day. 6/9/13

Adam (talking about playing the Spyro games): That
Moneybags is a greedy bastard. 6/13/13

Adam: When I said they needed to pave the road, I
meant it metaphorically. 6/13/13

Adam: Purple Heart Trail?! What kinda trail is
that? 6/13/13

Adam: That makes no sense. FREE with purchase?!
Just buy the cheapest thing possible. 6/14/13

Adam: It was either Mack or the ketchup bottle. It
didn't stink so I guess it was the ketchup.
6/14/13

Adam: You deserve to be pushed off a mountain.
6/30/2013

Adam: Can I have a sleepover at Grandma's? Me:
It's ok with me, but you need to call and ask her.
Adam: I might as well pack, cause Grandma won't
tell me no. 7/1/2013

Me: You are too dependent on technology. Adam:
Hey, I'm a kid of the 21st century. 7/16/2013

Adam: Mom is an Illinoisan. I meant that as a joke
and literally. 7/17/2013

Adam: Do you feel tired? I mean tired, tired, and
not tired of me? 7/26/2013

Adam: Are you going to vacuum today? Me: Yes.
Adam: Well, that's inconvenient. 7/28/2013

Adam: Will you take me to Walmart on October 13th?
Me: October 13th? Adam: That's specific, isn't it?
8/1/2013

Adam: Grandma is Uncle Tony's brother. 8/1/2013

Me: Grab that doorknob and walk backwards into the
hall. Goodbye! Adam: HAHAHAHA that was a good one!
11/10/2013

Adam: You like racing the train, don't you? Me:
Yes, I do. 11/14/2013

I got a breaking news text last night from WSMV
about a body being found in West Nashville.
Me: Well, Adam, aren't you glad we know that there
was a body found?
Adam: No. I'd rather they keep it a secret...
11/18/2013

Me: Where does your cup go? Adam: America? Me:
Incorrect answer. Adam: Lewisburg, TN? Me:
Incorrect Answer. Adam: Our dishwasher... it is in
America and in Lewisburg, TN, so I am right.

I just had a lengthy conversation with Adam about
leaving Santa hot chocolate, and if he has a
microwave in his sleigh to warm it up, and if he
knows how to make coffee and if he likes to watch
football on the weekends.

Adam: Christmas is coming! Me: And the geese are
getting fat. Adam: WHAT? 12/18/2013

Adam: Mack is watching space stuff. Me: I know,
and it's New Year's, I want to watch New Year's
stuff. Adam: But the earth is..... ahhhhh.
12/31/201

Mack: ... this Whirlpool... Adam: What about squirrel poo? 1/9/2014

Adam: Mom? Me: What? Adam: I love tacos... and you. Me: LOL. Adam: What, you're the best mom I got! 1/10/2014

Adam: Can we get a West Highland White Terrier? I read about them. Me: I don't think so. Adam, to Ainsley: She said maybe! 1/11/2014

Adam: Mom is depressed, confused and congested. I am the people whisperer. 1/12/2014

Adam has a cup of ice. He wants it to slowly thaw so he put it in the refrigerator. He said "I put it directly under the light bulb, that should work, right?" 1/13/2014

Adam: You confuse me in so many ways. 2/28/2014

Adam: You're cooking breakfast and doing laundry at the same time?! You're on a roll! Me: It's multi-tasking and you could do it too if you were a girl. 3/6/2014

Adam: You can't say it's a bad habit 'cause everyone has to fart. 5/1/2014

So Adam is apparently so disturbed by a video shown at school today that he won't even talk about it. All he will say is "puberty" and "hair". 5/13/2014

Adam: If I don't scoop it, I don't poop it. 6/12/2014

Adam: It feels like it was just tomorrow that I was 11. 6/13/2014

Adam: You know that Friday the 13th stuff? Me: Yes? Adam: Well, I don't believe in it. You create

your own luck in this crazy messed up world.
6/13/2014

Adam (talking about Father's Day) It would be good
if one person was here with us.... George Jones.
6/14/2014

Adam: I know all animals are unique, but what's
with platypuses? Or is it platypi? It's like a
duck and a beaver had a baby. And a brick. It's
rectangular shaped. 6/16/2014

Me: I smell like dog. Adam: That's my feet.
6/26/2014

Adam: Grandma is worried about them being
efficient on the road construction so she goes
around the other way. If they were worried about
being efficient, they'd put up a "road closed"
sign. 6/26/2014

Adam: I have a question about this cat...is he
feral? Is he sterile? Is he Meryl? 7/3/2014

Adam: Marty is the cat version of Miley Cyrus with
his tongue sticking out. 7/7/2014

Adam: Marty isn't a normal animal. He has six
nipples. 8/6/2014

As I begin to vacuum, Adam starts picking his
stuff up in the living room to put away. Ainsley
asks him what he is doing. "Don't you hear that
ominous sound?" is his reply. I love that boy!
8/10/2014

Adam: Apparently, Dizzy was secretly watching me
use the bathroom. 8/29/2014

Adam: I'm gonna be ugly next year. Me: Why? Adam:
Puberty.

Adam: Dizzy looks like a burnt sausage.

Me: You lied to granddaddy. Adam: It was for my own protection. 9/9/2014

Adam: My marshmallow took flight. 9/14/2014

Me: OMG, I can't see, the sun is crazy bright! Adam: In about 2.3 billion years, that won't be a problem. 9/22/2014

Adam: Well, there's another burglary. Me: Where? Adam: They say one happens every 15 seconds..... there's another one. 10/24/2014

Adam: One day kangaroos are going to take over the world. 10/24/2014

Adam: One thing I like to do in the mornings is watch My Little Pony. Don't judge me. 10/24/2014

Adam: Are we doing anything for Ainsley's birthday this weekend ? Me: I think she's going to Martin. Adam: That's more like a gift for us.

Adam: I love you.... No, I hate you.... Actually, I have moderate feelings for you.

Adam: People like me because I'm a great conversationalist. I'm good for the lonely.

Adam: I'm opening presents at 7am on Christmas day. Me: 9:00. Adam: I'll take pictures. 12/21/2014

Sitting here watching the Sunday political shows. The question asked was... Who was the last sitting President to visit Cuba? Adam said JFK and Cuba is pretty much in isolation. He was wrong about who it was, but it shows this kid thinks! 12/21/2014

Adam: I have Mexican toys! Me: Mexican toys? Adam: Yes, they were made in China! 12/23/2014

Me: When am I going to get your report card? Adam:
Just so you know, I love you. 1/12/2015

Me: I didn't raise a liar. Adam: You raised
Ainsley. 1/12/2015